MOLY

MOLY

Thom Gunn

FABER AND FABER
3 Queen Square London

First published in 1971
by Faber and Faber Limited
3 Queen Square London WC1
Printed in Great Britain by
Latimer Trend & Co Ltd Plymouth

ISBN 0 571 09650 6

for Mike and Bill,
  with love

Contents

When I was near the house of Circe, I met Hermes in the likeness of a young man, the down just showing on his face. He came up to me and took my hand, saying: 'Where are you going, alone, and ignorant of the way? Your men are shut up in Circe's sties, like wild boars in their lairs. But take heart, I will protect you and help you. Here is a herb, one of great virtue: keep it about you when you go to Circe's house.' As he spoke he pulled the herb out of the ground and showed it to me. The root was black, the flower was as white as milk; the gods call it Moly.

Rites of Passage

Something is taking place.
Horns bud bright in my hair.
My feet are turning hoof.
And Father, see my face
—Skin that was damp and fair
Is barklike and, feel, rough.

See Greytop how I shine.
I rear, break loose, I neigh
Snuffing the air, and harden
Towards a completion, mine.
And next I make my way
Adventuring through your garden.

My play is earnest now.
I canter to and fro.
My blood, it is like light.
Behind an almond bough,
Horns gaudy with its snow,
I wait live, out of sight.

All planned before my birth
For you, Old Man, no other,
Whom your groin's trembling warns.
I stamp upon the earth
A message to my mother.
And then I lower my horns.

Moly

Nightmare of beasthood, snorting, how to wake.
I woke. What beasthood skin she made me take?

Leathery toad that ruts for days on end,
Or cringing dribbling dog, man's servile friend,

Or cat that prettily pounces on its meat,
Tortures it hours, then does not care to eat:

Parrot, moth, shark, wolf, crocodile, ass, flea.
What germs, what jostling mobs there were in me.

These seem like bristles, and the hide is tough.
No claw or web here: each foot ends in hoof.

Into what bulk has method disappeared?
Like ham, streaked. I am gross—grey, gross, flap-eared.

The pale-lashed eyes my only human feature.
My teeth tear, tear. I am the snouted creature

That bites through anything, root, wire, or can.
If I was not afraid I'd eat a man.

Oh a man's flesh already is in mine.
Hand and foot poised for risk. Buried in swine.

I root and root, you think that it is greed,
It is, but I seek out a plant I need.

Direct me gods, whose changes are all holy,
To where it flickers deep in grass, the moly:

Cool flesh of magic in each leaf and shoot,
From milky flower to the black forked root.

From this fat dungeon I could rise to skin
And human title, putting pig within.

I push my big grey wet snout through the green,
Dreaming the flower I have never seen.

For Signs

1

In front of me, the palings of a fence
Throw shadows hard as board across the weeds;
The cracked enamel of a chicken bowl
Gleams like another moon; each clump of reeds
Is split with darkness and yet bristles whole.
The field survives, but with a difference.

2

And sleep like moonlight drifts and clings to shape.
My mind, which learns its freedom every day,
Sinks into vacancy but cannot rest.
While moonlight floods the pillow where it lay,
It walks among the past, weeping, obsessed,
Trying to master it and learn escape.

I dream: the real is shattered and combined,
Until the moon comes back into that sign
It stood in at my birth-hour; and I pass
Back to the field where, statued in the shine,
Someone is gazing upward from the grass
As if toward vaults that honeycomb the mind.

Slight figure in a wide black hat, whose hair
Massed and moon-coloured almost hides his face.
The thin white lips are dry, the eyes intense
Watching not thing, but lunar orgy, chase,
Trap, and cool fantasy of violence.
I recognize the pale long inward stare.

His tight young flesh is only on the top.
Beneath it, is an answering moon, at full,
Pitted with craters and with empty seas.
Dream mentor, I have been inside that skull,
I too have used those cindered passages.

But now the moon leaves Scorpio: I look up.

3

No, not inconstant, though it is called so.
For I have always found it waiting there,
Whether reduced to an invisible seed,
Or whether swollen again above the air
To rake the oubliettes of pain and greed
Opened at night in fellowship below.

It goes, and in its going it returns,
Cycle that I in part am governed by
And cannot understand where it is dark.
I lean upon the fence and watch the sky,
How light fills blinded socket and chafed mark.
It soars, hard, full, and edged, it coldly burns.

Justin

Waiting for her in some small park,
The lamplight's little world clasped round
By sweet rot and the autumn dark,
Once Justin found, or thought he found,
His live flesh flake like onion-skin
From finger-bones where it had held,
And saw the muscle fray within,
Peeling from joints that bunched and swelled.
    The waits had totalled in the shade,
And he had, unaware of debt
Or of expense, already paid
The cost of what he didn't get.
Might she be there? He could not see.
But waiting wears as hard as action,
And he perceived what he would be,
Transparent with dissatisfaction.

Phaedra in the Farm House

From sleep, before first light,
I hear slow-rolling churns
Clank over flags below.
Aches me. The room returns.
I hurt, I wake, I know
The cold dead end of night.

Here father. And here son.
What trust I live between.
But warmth here on the sheet
Is kin-warmth, slow and clean.
I cook the food two eat,
But oh, I sleep with one.

And you, in from the stable.
You spent last evening
Lost in the chalky blues
Of warm hills, rabbitting.
You frown and spell the news,
With forearms on the table.

Tonight, though, we play cards.
You are not playing well.
I smell the oil-lamp's jet,
The parlour's polished smell,
Then you—soap, ghost of sweat,
Tractor oil, and the yards.

Shirt-sleeved you concentrate.
Your moleskin waistcoat glints.

Your quick grin never speaks:
I study you for hints
—Hints from those scrubbed boy-cheeks?

I deal a grown man's fate.

The churns wait on in mud:
Tomorrow's milk will sour.
I leave, but bit by bit,
Sharp through the last whole hour.
The chimney will be split,
And that waistcoat be blood.

The Sand Man

Tourists in summer, looking at the view,
    The Bay, the Gate, the Bridge,
From sands that, yearly, city trucks renew,
    Descry him at the postcard's edge.

A white-haired man who hauls up lengths of wood
    And lies beside his fire
Motionless on his side, or gumming food,
    Without a thought, or much desire.

After the beating, thirty-five years since,
    A damaged consciousness
Reduced itself to that mere innocence
    Many have tried to repossess.

Bare to the trunks, the body on the ground
    Is sun-stained, ribbed, and lean:
And slowly in the sand rolls round and round
    In patient reperformed routine.

Sand, sticking to him, keeps him from the dust,
    And armours him about.
Now covered, he has entered that old trust,
    Like sandflies when the tide is out.

He rocks, a blur on ridges, pleased to be.
    Dispersing with the sands
He feels a dry cool multiplicity
    Gilding his body, feet and hands.

Apartment Cats

The Girls wake, stretch, and pad up to the door.
    They rub my leg and purr:
    One sniffs around my shoe,
    Rich with an outside smell,
  The other rolls back on the floor—
White bib exposed, and stomach of soft fur.

Now, more awake, they re-enact Ben Hur
    Along the corridor,
    Wheel, gallop; as they do,
    Their noses twitching still,
  Their eyes get wild, their bodies tense,
Their usual prudence seemingly withdraws.

And then they wrestle: parry, lock of paws,
    Blind hug of close defence,
    Tail-thump, and smothered mew.
    If either, though, feel claws,
  She abruptly rises, knowing well
How to stalk off in wise indifference.

Three

All three are bare.
The father towels himself by two grey boulders
  Long body, then long hair,
Matted like rainy bracken, to his shoulders.

    The pull and risk
Of the Pacific's touch is yet with him:
  He kicked and felt it brisk,
Its cold live sinews tugging at each limb.

    It haunts him still:
Drying his loins, he grins to notice how,
  Struck helpless with the chill,
His cock hangs tiny and withdrawn there now.

    Near, eyes half-closed,
The mother lies back on the hot round stones,
  Her weight to theirs opposed
And pressing them as if they were earth's bones.

    Hard bone, firm skin,
She holds her breasts and belly up, now dry,
  Striped white where clothes have been,
To the heat that sponsors all heat, from the sky.

    Only their son
Is brown all over. Rapt in endless play,
  In which all games make one,
His three-year nakedness is everyday.

Swims as dogs swim.
Rushes his father, wriggles from his hold.
　His body, which is him,
Sturdy and volatile, runs off the cold.

　　Runs up to me:
Hi there hi there, he shrills, yet will not stop,
　For though continually
Accepting everything his play turns up

　　He still leaves it
And comes back to that pebble-warmed recess
　In which the parents sit,
At watch, who had to learn their nakedness.

Words

The shadow of a pine-branch quivered
On a sunlit bank of pale unflowering weed.
  I watched, more solid by the pine,
The dark exactitude that light delivered,
    And, from obsession, or from greed,
      Laboured to make it mine.

  In looking for the words, I found
Bright tendrils, round which that sharp outline faltered:
  Limber detail, no bloom disclosed.
I was still separate on the shadow's ground
    But, charged with growth, was being altered,
      Composing uncomposed.

From the Wave

It mounts at sea, a concave wall
    Down-ribbed with shine,
And pushes forward, building tall
    Its steep incline.

Then from their hiding rise to sight
    Black shapes on boards
Bearing before the fringe of white
    It mottles towards.

Their pale feet curl, they poise their weight
    With a learn'd skill.
It is the wave they imitate
    Keeps them so still.

The marbling bodies have become
    Half wave, half men,
Grafted it seems by feet of foam
    Some seconds, then,

Late as they can, they slice the face
    In timed procession:
Balance is triumph in this place,
    Triumph possession.

The mindless heave of which they rode
    A fluid shelf
Breaks as they leave it, falls and, slowed,
    Loses itself.

Clear, the sheathed bodies slick as seals
    Loosen and tingle;
And by the board the bare foot feels
    The suck of shingle.

They paddle in the shallows still;
    Two splash each other;
Then all swim out to wait until
    The right waves gather.

Tom-Dobbin

1

light is in the pupil
                   luminous seed
and light is in the mind
                       crossing
in an instant
               passage between the two
seamless
           imperceptible transition
skin melting downward into hide
at the centaur's waist
                  there is the one
and at once it is also the other

fair freckled skin, the blond down on it
being at all points
               a beginning
to the glossy chestnut brown which
is also at all points
                a beginning upward

2

Hot in his mind, Tom watches Dobbin fuck,
Watches, and smiles with pleasure, oh what luck.
He sees beyond, and knows he sees, red cows,
Harsh green of grass, and pink-fired chestnut boughs.
The great brown body rears above the mare,
Plunging beneath Tom's interested stare.

In coming Tom and Dobbin join to one——
Only a moment, just as it is done:
A shock of whiteness, shooting like a star,
In which all colours of the spectrum are.

3

He grins, he plunges into orgy. It moves about him in easy eddies, and he enters their mingling and branching. He spreads with them, he is veined with sunshine.

The cobalt gleam of a peacock's neck, the course of a wind through grasses, distant smoke frozen in the sky, are extensions of self.

And later something in him rises, neither sun nor moon, close and brilliant. It lights the debris, and brings it all together. It grins too, with its own concentrating passion. It discovers dark shining tables of rock that rise, inch by inch, out of the turning waters.

4

The mammal is with her young. She is unique.
Millions of years ago mixed habits gave
That crisp perfected outline, webs, fur, beak.

Risen from her close tunnel to her cave
The duck-billed platypus lies in ripeness till
The line of her belly breaks into a dew.
The brown fur oozes milk for the young one. He,
Hatched into separation, beaks his fill.
If you could see through darkness you could see
One breaking outline that includes the two.

5

Ruthlessly gentle, gently ruthless we move
As if through water with delaying limb.
We circle clasping round an unmarked centre
Gradually closing in, until we enter
The haze together—which is me, which him?
Selves floating in the one flesh we are of.

The Rooftop

White houses bank the hill,
Facing me where I sit.
It should be adequate
To watch the gardens fill

With sunlight, washing tree,
Bush, and the year's last flowers,
And to sit here for hours,
Becoming what I see.

Perception gave me this:
A whole world, bit by bit.
Yet I can not grasp it—
Bits, not an edifice.

Long webs float on the air.
Glistening, they fall and lift.
I turn it down, the gift:
Such fragile lights can tear.

The heat frets earth already,
Harrowed by furious root;
The wireworm takes his loot;
The midday sun is steady.

Petals turn brown and splay:
Loose in a central shell
Seeds whitening dry and swell
Which light fills from decay.

Ruthless in clean unknowing
The plant obeys its need,
And works alone. The seed
Bursts, bare as bone in going,

Bouncing from rot toward earth,
Compound of rot, to wait,
An armoured concentrate
Containing its own birth.

An unseen edifice.
The seen, the tangles, lead
From seed to death to seed
Through green closed passages.

The light drains from the hill.
The gardens rustle, cold,
Huddled in dark, and hold,
Waiting for when they fill.

The Colour Machine

1

Suddenly it is late night, there are people
in the basement, we all sit and lie in front of the
colour machine. Someone among us, at the controls,
switches to green and red. Now the shape in it is
riding through a dark red-green sea, it is like matter
approaching and retreating from the brink of form.
Where it has thickened it starts to turn transparent;
where it is almost transparent it starts to thicken.
We cannot tell what it reminds us of: it is in a state
of unending alteration: we can name it only afterwards.

2

Giving himself completely to the colour machine,
one of us became invisible. Being a thing, it does not
need gifts, and anyway what wants something that
becomes invisible as soon as given? It let him go, and he
drifted from the room into a world where he could no
longer make an impression: plants grew into the bridge
of his foot, cars drove through him, he entered movies for
free. And of course, we never saw him again.

I too am a lover, but I am cowardly, selfish, and
calculating. When I most long to give myself, heart,
body, and mind, to the colour machine, I remember our
friend, give a mocking smile, and start making love to
curtains. By means of such promiscuity I can keep myself
intact. But I am uneasy, and hanker for courage and
impulsiveness. Perhaps, for our vanished friend, the
moment of giving made the fact of his disintegration

35

something of negligible importance. Or perhaps his consciousness still lives in the intensity of that moment. I am visible and do not know.

1965

Street Song

I am too young to grow a beard
But yes man it was me you heard
In dirty denim and dark glasses.
I look through everyone who passes
But ask him clear, I do not plead,
Keys lids acid and speed.

My grass is not oregano.
Some of it grew in Mexico.
You cannot guess the weed I hold,
Clara Green, Acapulco Gold,
Panama Red, you name it man,
Best on the street since I began.

My methedrine, my double-sun,
Will give you two lives in your one,
Five days of power before you crash.
At which time use these lumps of hash
—They burn so sweet, they smoke so smooth,
They make you sharper while they soothe.

Now here, the best I've got to show,
Made by a righteous cat I know.
Pure acid—it will scrape your brain,
And make it something else again.
Call it heaven, call it hell,
Join me and see the world I sell.

Join me, and I will take you there,
Your head will cut out from your hair
Into whichever self you choose.
With Midday Mick man you can't lose,
I'll get you anything you need.
Keys lids acid and speed.

The Fair in the Woods

to Jere Fransway

The woodsmen blow their horns, and close the day,
Grouped by some logs. The buckskins they are in
Merge with ground's russet and with tree-trunk's grey,
And through the colour of the body's skin
Shift borrowings out of nearby birch and clay.

All day a mounted angel came and went
Sturdily pacing through the trees and crowd,
His horse glossy and obedient.
Points glowed among his hair: dark-haired, dark-browed.
He supervised a god's experiment.

Some clustered in the upper boughs, from where
They watched the groups beneath them make their way,
Children of light, all different, through the fair,
Pulsing among the pulsing trunks. And they,
The danglers, ripened in the brilliant air.

Upon a platform dappled by the sun
The whole speed-family in a half round clapped
About the dancer where she arched and spun.
They raced toward stillness till they overlapped,
Ten energies working inward through the one.

Landscape of acid:
                    where on fern and mound
The lights fragmented by the roofing bough
Throbbed outward, joining over broken ground
To one long dazzling burst; as even now
Horn closes over horn into one sound.

Knuckle takes back its colour, nail its line.
Slowly the tawny jerkins separate
From bark and earth, but they will recombine
In the autumnal dusk, for it is late.
The horns call. There is little left to shine.

LSD, San Rafael Woods: 'Renaissance Fair'

Listening to Jefferson Airplane
in the Polo Grounds, Golden Gate Park

The music comes and goes on the wind,
Comes and goes on the brain.

To Natty Bumppo

The grey eyes watchful and a lightened hand.
The ruder territory opening up
Fills with discovery: unoutlined land
With which familiar places overlap.

A feeling forward, or a being aware.
I reach, out, on: beyond the elm-topped rise
There is, not yet but forming now, a there
To be completed by the opened eyes.

A plain, a forest, a field full of folk.
Footing the sun-shot turf beneath the trees,
They brandish their arms upward like the oak,
Their sky-blue banners rest along the breeze.

Open on all sides, it is held in common,
The first field of a glistening continent
Each found by trusting Eden in the human:
The guiding hand, the bright grey eyes intent.

The Garden of the Gods

All plants grow here; the most minute,
  Glowing from turf, is in its place.
  The constant vision of the race:
Lawned orchard deep with flower and fruit.

So bright, that some who see it near,
  Think there is lapis on the stems,
  And think green, blue, and crimson gems
Hang from the vines and briars here.

They follow path to path in wonder
  Through the intense undazzling light.
  Nowhere does blossom flare so white!
Nowhere so black is earthmould under!

It goes, though it may come again.
  But if at last they try to tell,
  They search for trope or parallel,
And cannot, after all, explain.

It was sufficient, there, to be,
  And meaning, thus, was superseded.
  —Night circles it, it has receded,
Distant and difficult to see.

Where my foot rests, I hear the creak
  From generations of my kin,
  Layer on layer, pressed leaf-thin.
They merely are. They cannot speak.

This was the garden's place of birth:
   I trace it downward from my mind,
   Through breast and calf I feel it vined,
And rooted in the death-rich earth.

Flooded Meadows

In sunlight now, after the weeks it rained,
Water has mapped irregular shapes that follow
Between no banks, impassive where it drained
Then stayed to rise and brim from every hollow.
Hillocks are firm, though soft, and not yet mud.
Tangles of long bright grass, like waterweed,
Surface upon the patches of the flood,
Distinct as islands from their valleys freed
And sharp as reefs dividing inland seas.
Yet definition is suspended, for,
In pools across the level listlessness,
Light answers only light before the breeze,
Cancelling the rutted, weedy, slow brown floor
For the unity of unabsorbed excess.

Grasses

Laurel and eucalyptus, dry sharp smells,
Pause in the dust of summer. But we sit
High on a fort, above grey blocks and wells,
And watch the restless grasses lapping it.

Each dulling-green, keen, streaky blade of grass
Leans to one body when the breezes start:
A one-time pathway flickers as they pass,
Where paler toward the root the quick ranks part.

The grasses quiver, rising from below.
I wait on warm rough concrete, I have time.
They round off all the lower steps, and blow
Like lights on bended water as they climb.

From some dark passage in the abandoned fort,
I hear a friend's harmonica—withdrawn sound,
A long whine drawling after several short . . .
The spiky body mounting from the ground.

A wail uneven all the afternoon,
Thin, slow, no noise of tramping nor of dance.
It is the sound, half tuneless and half tune,
With which the scattered details make advance.

Kirby's Cove

The Messenger

Is this man turning angel as he stares
At one red flower whose name he does not know,
   The velvet face, the black-tipped hairs?

His eyes dilated like a cat's at night,
His lips move somewhat but he does not speak
   Of what completes him through his sight.

His body makes to imitate the flower,
Kneeling, with splayed toes pushing at the soil,
   The source, crude, granular, and sour.

His stillness answers like a looking glass
The flower's, it is repose of unblown flame
   That nests within the glow of grass.

Later the news, to branch from sense and sense,
Bringing their versions of the flower in small
   Outward into intelligence.

But meanwhile, quiet and reaching as a flame,
He bends, gazing not at but into it,
   Tough stalk, and face without a name.

Being Born

The tanker slips behind a distant ridge
And, on the blue, a formal S of smoke
Still hangs. I send myself out on my look.
But just beyond my vision, at the edge

To left and right, there reach or seem to reach
Margins, vague pillars, not quite visible,
Or unfleshed giant presences so tall
They stretch from top to bottom, sky to beach.

What memory loosed, of man and boundary blended?
One tug, one more, and I could have it here.
—Yes that's it, ah two shapes begin to clear:
Midwife and doctor faintly apprehended.

I let them both almost solidify,
Their quiet activity bit by bit outlined,
Clean hand and calm eye, but still view behind,
Bright crinkling foam, headland, and level sky.

I think of being grabbed from the warm sand,
Shiny red bawling newborn with clenched eyes,
Slapped into life; and as it clarifies
My friends recede, alas the dwindling land.

Must I rewrite my childhood? What jagg'd growth
What mergings of authority and pain,
Invading breath, must I live through again?
Are they the past or yet to come or both?

Both. Between moving air and moving ocean
The tanker pushes, squat and purposeful,
But elsewhere. And the smoke. Though now air's pull
Begins to suck it into its own motion.

There is a furnace that connects them there.
The metal, guided, cuts through fall and lift,
While the coils from it widen, spread, and drift
To feed the open currents of the air.

At the Centre

1

What place is this
                  Cracked wood steps led me here.
The gravelled roof is fenced in where I stand.
But it is open, I am not confined
By weathered boards or barbed wire at the stair,
From which rust crumbles black-red on my hand.
If it is mine. It looks too dark and lined.

What sky
         A pearly damp grey covers it
Almost infringing on the lighted sign
Above Hamm's Brewery, a huge blond glass
Filling as its component lights are lit.
You cannot keep them. Blinking line by line
They brim beyond the scaffold they replace.

2

What is this steady pouring that
                        Oh, wonder.
The blue line bleeds and on the gold one draws.
Currents of image widen, braid, and blend
—Pouring in cascade over me and under—
To one all-river. Fleet it does not pause,
The sinewy flux pours without start or end.

What place is this
                And what is it that broods
Barely beyond its own creation's course,

And not abstracted from it, not the Word,
But overlapping like the wet low clouds
The rivering images—their unstopped source,
Its roar unheard from being always heard.

What am
                    Though in the river, I abstract
Fence, word, and notion. On the stream at full
A flurry, where the mind rides separate!
But this brief cresting, sharpened and exact,
Is fluid too, is open to the pull
And on the underside twined deep with it.

3

Terror and beauty in a single board.
The rough grain in relief—a tracery
Fronded and ferned, of woods inside the wood.
Splinter and scar—I saw them too, they poured.
White paint-chip and the overhanging sky:
The flow-lines faintly traced or understood.

Later, downstairs and at the kitchen table,
I look round at my friends. Through light we move
Like foam. We started choosing long ago
—Clearly and capably as we were able—
Hostages from the pouring we are of.
The faces are as bright now as fresh snow.

                              LSD, Folsom Street

The Discovery of the Pacific

They lean against the cooling car, backs pressed
Upon the dusts of a brown continent,
And watch the sun, now Westward of their West,
Fall to the ocean. Where it led they went.

Kansas to California. Day by day
They travelled emptier of the things they knew.
They improvised new habits on the way,
But lost the occasions, and then lost them too.

One night, no-one and nowhere, she had woken
To resin-smell and to the firs' slight sound,
And through their sleeping-bag had felt the broken
Tight-knotted surfaces of the naked ground.

Only his lean quiet body cupping hers
Kept her from it, the extreme chill. By degrees
She fell asleep. Around them in the firs
The wind probed, tiding through forked estuaries.

And now their skin is caked with road, the grime
Merely reflecting sunlight as it fails.
They leave their clothes among the rocks they climb,
Blunt leaves of iceplant nuzzle at their soles.

Now they stand chin-deep in the sway of ocean,
Firm West, two stringy bodies face to face,
And come, together, in the water's motion,
The full caught pause of their embrace.

Sunlight

Some things, by their affinity light's token,
Are more than shown: steel glitters from a track;
Small glinting scoops, after a wave has broken,
Dimple the water in its draining back;

Water, glass, metal, match light in their raptures,
Flashing their many answers to the one.
What captures light belongs to what it captures:
The whole side of a world facing the sun,

Re-turned to woo the original perfection,
Giving itself to what created it,
And wearing green in sign of its subjection.
It is as if the sun were infinite.

But angry flaws are swallowed by the distance;
It varies, moves, its concentrated fires
Are slowly dying—the image of persistence
Is an image, only, of our own desires:

Desires and knowledge touch without relating.
The system of which sun and we are part
Is both imperfect and deteriorating.
And yet the sun outlasts us at the heart.

Great seedbed, yellow centre of the flower,
Flower on its own, without a root or stem,
Giving all colour and all shape their power,
Still recreating in defining them,

Enable us, altering like you, to enter
Your passionless love, impartial but intense,
And kindle in acceptance round your centre,
Petals of light lost in your innocence.

Acknowledgements

The poems in this book first appeared in the following
publications: *The Listener, Ambit, Antaeus, Art and Artists,
London Magazine, Poetry Review*, and *Tri Quarterly*.
Some were broadcast on the BBC, and some
appeared in pamphlets published by the Albondocani
Press, Richard Gilbertson, the Pym-Randall Press and
the Sycamore Press. 'The Messenger', 'Being Born' and
'The Discovery of the Pacific' were first published in
Poetry. 'Rites of Passage', 'For Signs', 'Justin' and
'Words' were first published in the *Southern Review*.